Grow Grateful

By Sage Foster-Lasser
and Jon Lasser, PhD

Illustrated by
Christopher Lyles

Magination Press • Washington, DC • American Psychological Association

American Psychological Association
750 First Street NE
Washington, DC 20002

Book design by Gwen Grafft
Printed by Lake Book Manufacturing, Inc., Melrose Park, IL

Library of Congress Cataloging-in-Publication Data
Names: Foster-Lasser, Sage, author. | Lasser, Jon (Psychology professor),
    author. | Lyles, Christopher, 1977– illustrator.
Title: Grow grateful / by Sage Foster-Lasser and Jon Lasser, PhD ;
    illustrated by Christopher Lyles.
Description: Washington, DC : Magination Press, [2018] | Audience: Age: 4–8.
Identifiers: LCCN 2017046494| ISBN 9781433829031 (hardcover) | ISBN
    1433829037 (hardcover)
Subjects: LCSH: Gratitude—Juvenile literature. | Children—Conduct of life.
Classification: LCC BF575.G68 F67 2018 | DDC 179/.9—dc23
LC record available at https://lccn.loc.gov/2017046494

Manufactured in the United States of America
10 9 8 7 6 5 4 3 2

I'm Kiko.
I'm a happy camper!
I can grow grateful, too.
Let me show you how.

My class goes on lots of field trips. Ms. Cooper
has taken us to the art museum, the state capitol,
and even to a bakery, but never camping.
I was excited! I counted the days until we left!

Do you want to know something else?
Part of me was nervous about camping, too.

When I asked my dad what he was bringing for us to eat, he told me that he and my mom weren't going.

"Why not?"

"Well, this trip is for you, Jasmine, and all your classmates and Ms. Cooper. Besides, someone has to look out for Chico."

My dad bent down, scooped me up, and
tossed me high in the air as I squealed.

"Not so high!"

I was thankful that someone would be there to keep Chico company.

My brother Nick told me about the trip from
when he was in Ms. Cooper's class.

"It was so much fun. We had a campfire and ate
marshmallows! We climbed to the top of Cactus Ridge!"

"Cactus Ridge? Is it high? Is it steep?"

"Very high. Very steep."

I was happy Jasmine would be there. She doesn't like heights either.

When we got to the camping site, I peeked into my backpack filled with my water bottle and snacks my dad packed for me.

Yummy! My dad knows what I like and packed the most delicious snacks—green grapes and very berry granola! And some chocolate chip cookies. I shared my snacks with Jasmine.

All the kids were divided into two groups, the Bluebirds and the Sparrows. Jasmine was a Bluebird, and I was a Sparrow! The Bluebirds would hike up the east side of Cactus Ridge, and the Sparrows would climb the west side.

I got nervous again, imagining climbing all that way without Jasmine. But I noticed Camille. She looked scared, too.

"It's okay, Camille," I told her. "I don't like heights either, so we can stick together."

Helping Camille helped me feel better, too. My gratitude was growing!

We walked hand in hand, step by step. At one point, I tried to touch the soft flower petal of a prickly pear and felt a sharp pain in my finger. Ms. Cooper removed the cactus spine from my finger with her tweezers. I was relieved that she was there to help me.

When we finally reached the top,
I couldn't believe how beautiful the
view was. I was proud that Camille
and I had helped each other. Soon after
we reached the top, I saw Jasmine's
head pop out from the other side of the
rock. I waved excitedly at her.

As the sun began to set, we pitched our tents. After we all ate dinner, we built a fire to sit around. As we were roasting our marshmallows, Ms. Cooper said,

"Let's each go around and say what we're most grateful for tonight."

Moseah asked, "What does grateful mean?"

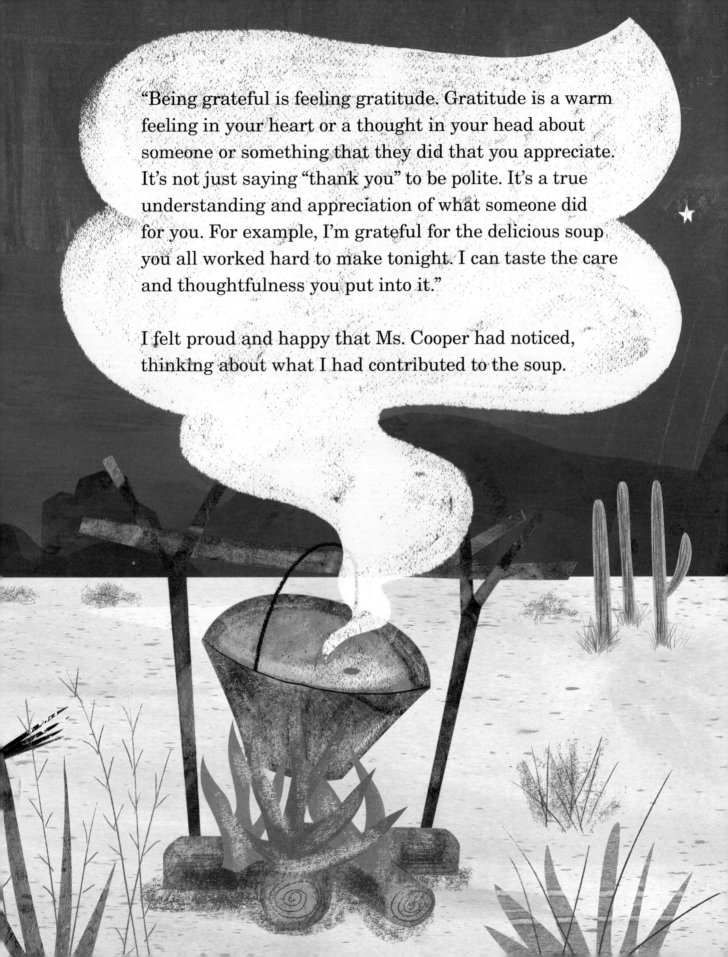

"Being grateful is feeling gratitude. Gratitude is a warm feeling in your heart or a thought in your head about someone or something that they did that you appreciate. It's not just saying "thank you" to be polite. It's a true understanding and appreciation of what someone did for you. For example, I'm grateful for the delicious soup you all worked hard to make tonight. I can taste the care and thoughtfulness you put into it."

I felt proud and happy that Ms. Cooper had noticed, thinking about what I had contributed to the soup.

Everyone was grateful for different things.

Emma for the colorful sunset over the mountains.

Margaret for the care package her parents sent for us.

Moseah for the gorgeous hawk that had circled over his head.

Jasmine for the toasted marshmallows.

Camille for a friend to keep her company along the steep ridge!

That night as I fell asleep, I thought about my parents and how nice it was that they sent me on this trip. I thought about Camille and Jasmine and Ms. Cooper. The super steep ridge, the beautiful view, and the warm campfire.

I felt happy in my heart, just like
Ms. Cooper said. I had gratitude.

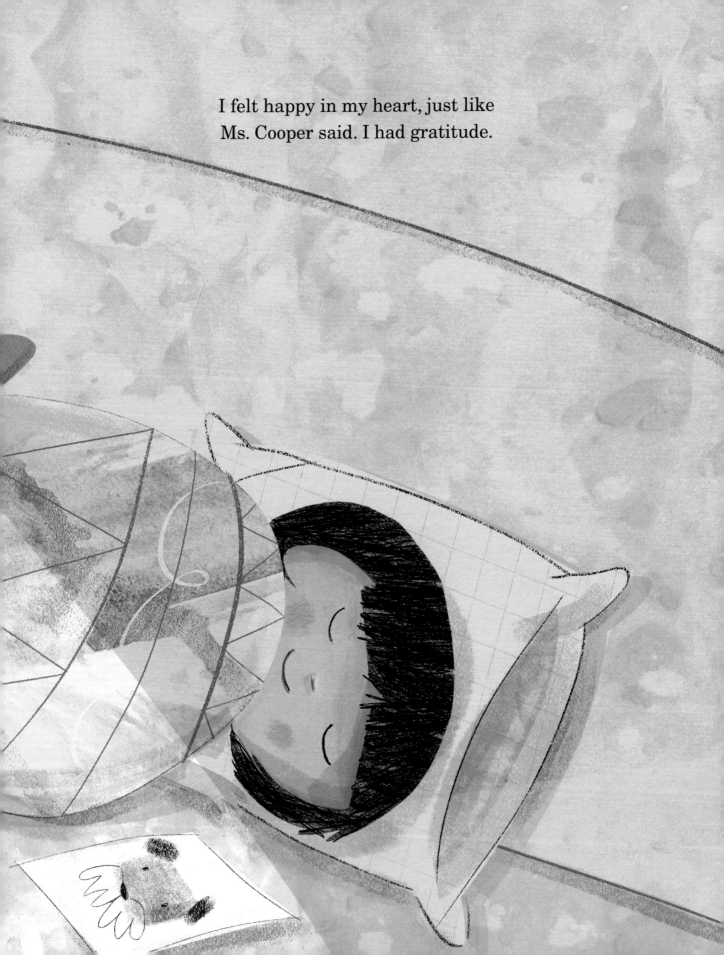

When I got home, I was so happy to see Chico and my family. I told them all about the trip and how grateful I was for the experience.

Dad was so happy to see me that he whisked me up in the air above his head, but this time I wasn't so scared.

How do you grow grateful?

Reader's Note

"Let us be grateful to the people who make us happy; they are the charming gardeners who make our souls blossom." —Marcel Proust

Gratitude is a complex experience of thoughts and feelings that we have in relationships with others. Psychologists believe that gratitude is an important part of our overall well-being and that having gratitude leads to greater happiness and better interpersonal relationships. Young children learn gratitude as they develop socially, cognitively, and emotionally. This book was written to help children learn about their own gratitude and that of others as part of their social-emotional learning.

Most children develop thoughts and feelings related to gratitude through social learning (i.e., observing gratitude expressed by others) and by having their own experiences of gratitude. This book, set around a camping trip, facilitates the development of gratitude by providing examples with fun characters with whom children can identify. Moreover, *Grow Grateful* builds children's vocabulary by introducing the words and concepts of "grateful" and "gratitude."

How to Use This Book

Grow Grateful is based in part on an idea that psychologists call "theory of mind," which is the ability to take the perspective of others. Most children begin to recognize around age 4-5 that each person has their own thoughts, feelings, and perspective (though this recognition may develop later in some). Once our capacity to think about the intentions, motivations, and goals of others emerges, we have a greater ability to experience gratitude.

The development of gratitude also emerges with children's moral development. Along with physical growth and language development comes greater sophistication in evaluating the behaviors of others and making value judgments. Coupled with the growth in perspective-taking, this newly developed moral reasoning allows children to think about what others may have done for them and consequently experience gratitude for others.

Grow Grateful shows children that when we are helpful to others, we are appreciated. Similarly, when others help us, we are grateful. The story revolves around a camping trip because such adventures frequently engender multiple feelings, including excitement, deprivation, and compassion. Feelings of hurt, loss, or deprivation that are met with compassion for others foster increased gratitude. Making sense of these feelings and how we experience the behaviors and feelings of others helps us develop a greater sense of gratitude.

After reading this book to your child, you might want to try some of these conversation starters. Listen to your child's responses without evaluating or judging them. Sometimes the best response from an adult is simply to repeat back what the child said (or paraphrase their response) to show that you heard and understood them. These conversation starters were designed to promote thoughts about gratitude, so there are no right or wrong answers. Give these a try:

"I'm grateful that I have you in my life because you're a wonderful child. What makes you feel grateful?" By providing an example of your own gratitude, you're modeling for your child how you express your feelings. Don't be surprised if they respond in a very concrete way ("I'm grateful for this toy I'm holding") or if they replicate your example. The emphasis here should be on learning how to identify thoughts and feelings of gratitude, and over time your child's understanding of this will become more elaborate. Try to include something about your child that is unique or specific to them.

"I feel grateful when someone does something nice for me. Can you think of a time that someone did something nice for you? What was it? How did it make you feel?" Young children may have a hard time grasping an abstract idea like gratitude, as they are better able to think in concrete terms. However, you can facilitate their development of gratitude by pointing to lived examples. Better yet, encourage them to recall situations in which someone was helpful to them. If they have a hard time identifying such situations, consider providing an example (e.g., "remember when you forgot your lunch and Grandma brought it to school?"). After the memory is identified, encourage your child to focus on the feelings associated with that memory.

"I feel great when I get to help people. It makes me happy! Let's think of someone that we can help. Do you have any ideas?" By encouraging your child to be helpful to others, you're helping them view service as a way to grow happiness. Allow your child to come up with an idea of someone that can be helped, and then put that idea into action (your child may need some help with this). If your child's idea is not practical, gently suggest something that seems feasible. This may also be a good opportunity to facilitate your child's growing capacity to take the perspectives of others.

"I wonder how _____ will feel after you help him/her?" During early childhood, there are a limited number of words that are used to describe feelings (e.g., happy, sad, mad). Many children will report that someone will feel happy after being helped. A good response to this, which may also help develop a more expansive vocabulary, may be, "Yes, she will feel happy after we help her. I'm sure she'll feel grateful too!" By reading the book and then talking about feelings of gratitude with your child, the concept will begin to come to life. Don't be surprised if your child starts talking about feeling grateful as you identify examples in your lives.

How to Help Your Child

There are lots of ways that adults can help children develop the cognitive, social, and emotional foundations of gratitude. The suggestions below can be adjusted to meet the varying developmental needs of children (e.g., an activity that calls for writing can be accomplished by drawing a picture or having the child dictate to the parent).

Foster authentic gratitude. Gratitude isn't meaningful when it's not authentic, so try to avoid forcing expressions of thankfulness. Instead, encourage thoughtful reflection and allow grateful feelings to emerge. Rather than instructing your child to say thank you after a home-cooked meal, talk to them about the farming, cooking, and preparation processes that went into creating the meal. In this way, you can help your child evoke more genuine feelings of gratitude.

Create grateful art. Get out some art materials and work with your child to make something creative around the theme of gratitude. For example, you and your child can cut out pictures from old magazines that represent things for which you are grateful and then glue the pictures to poster board. You can hang up your gratitude collage as a reminder of the things for which you're thankful. When doing this, let your child select his or her own pictures without direction from you, as gratitude is individualized and personal.

Make a gratitude visit. This idea is adapted from the work of Dr. Martin Seligman, a professor of psychology at the University of Pennsylvania. Encourage your child to think of someone who has been kind and helpful to them. It may be a family member, a teacher, a neighbor, etc. Then ask your child to write (or dictate) a letter about how that person was helpful. Finally, take your child to deliver the letter of gratitude. This activity promotes not only reflection, but also the expression of feelings.

Volunteer with your child. Select a community volunteer project that welcomes children, and spend some time engaged in helping others with your child. You and your child are likely to meet new people, be helpful, and experience the gratitude of others. Explain to your child that helping others is a fun way to share your time. You can find volunteer opportunities in your area at Serve.gov.

Express your gratitude as an example. When children hear our thoughts and feelings, they learn about verbalizing internal states. The goal here is to help children understand that we can communicate to others what's going on inside, including feeling grateful. At dinner, you might say, "I'm so grateful for the farmer who grew this delicious broccoli!" As we mentioned earlier, gratitude ought to be authentic, so express it only when you're really feeling it. Similarly, don't place an expectation on children to reciprocate. They'll express their gratitude when they feel it and are ready to share it.

Talk about how kindness makes others feel. Suppose you and your child are baking a cake for a family member. Encourage your child to predict how the recipient of the cake will feel. You might ask your child, "How will Mommy feel when we give this cake to her? What will she think?" To add a bit of humor, consider asking, "How would she feel if we gave her a dirty old shoe instead? What would she think?" The purpose of this is to facilitate your child's growth around perspective-taking and predicting the reactions of others. If we can learn how to behave in such a way that brings others joy, we can promote greater gratitude.

Identify gratitude when you see it. Once you start looking for examples of gratitude, you're likely to see it everywhere. You can help your child by pointing out signs of kindness, helpful behaviors, and appreciation. Point out gratitude when you see it at the park, in books, at home, and at the grocery store. Encourage your child to look for signs of gratitude out in the world. You may cue them to look not only for things people say, but also facial expressions and body language.

Not feeling so grateful? Sometimes it's hard to feel grateful, particularly when things are not going well in our lives. This is understandable, and we should avoid judging children who do not express gratitude. Should a child exhibit chronic irritability or a pervasive state of negative affect, you may consult a psychologist to determine whether professional help is needed. When a child experiences negative emotions, adults sometimes have a tendency to push those feelings away, but what children need most is to be certain that they are loved and understood.

About the Authors

Sage Foster-Lasser is an undergraduate student at the University of Texas at Austin, where she studies psychology and American studies. *Grow Grateful* is a follow-up to *Grow Happy*, her first children's book which she also co-authored with Jon. Sage is grateful for her wonderful family and friends, the beautiful city she lives in, and her fabulous dog, Nico.

Jon Lasser, PhD, is a psychologist, school psychologist, professor, and associate dean for research in the College of Education at Texas State University. *Grow Grateful* is a follow up to his first children's book, *Grow Happy*, also written with Sage. He's grateful for family, friends, and tacos. Jon Lasser resides in Martindale, Texas.

About the Illustrator

Christopher Lyles has illustrated numerous books for children. Inspired by vintage graphics and antique surfaces, he uses collage and mixed media applications to create his art. He lives in Simsbury, CT, a quiet New England town surrounded by wilderness. When he is not creating picture books, he enjoys spending time with his family and hiking the surrounding woods.

About Magination Press

Magination Press is an imprint of the American Psychological Association, the largest scientific and professional organization representing psychologists in the United States and the largest association of psychologists worldwide.